AWKWARD ANNIE

AWKWARD ANNIE

by Julia Williams
and Tim Archbold

Evans

First published 2007
Evans Brothers Limited
2A Portman Mansions
Chiltern St
London WIU 6NR

British Library Cataloguing in Publication Data

Williams, Julia
  Awkward Annie. - (Skylarks)
  1. Children's stories
  I. Title II. Archbold, Tim
  823.9'2[J]

  ISBN-13: 9780237533847 (hb)
  ISBN-13: 9780237534028 (pb)
Printed in China by WKT Co. Ltd

Series Editor: Louise John
Design: Robert Walster
Production: Jenny Mulvanny

Contents

Chapter One

Awkward Annie – that's what my mum
and dad call me. Well, not all the time.
When I'm being nice, Dad calls me
Beautiful Bella, on account of my full
name being Annabelle. But that's not
too often. Apparently middle children
are often awkward – at least that's what
I heard Awful Aunt Aggie saying loudly
once to Mum. Mum shut her up pretty
quickly, but… still. How would you like
it if people thought you were awkward?

I don't think I'm awkward. Not really.
I never mean to be awkward. And I tell
you what, you'd be awkward too, with a
family like mine.

First there's my really, really horrible big sister Posy. Perfect Posy I call her. Because she is. Perfect that is. She never has a hair out of place. She always gets ten out of ten in her spelling tests, she knows her times tables up to one hundred, and she never ever gets into trouble. Plus she's always neat and tidy,

so Mum never shouts at her. Sometimes I just hate having her for a big sister. And she makes it worse by always being so nice to me.

Then there's Ant, my annoying little brother. He's three years old and the BIGGEST pain. He scribbles on all my pictures, splashes me in the bath, and pulls the legs off my dolls. He also runs around and shouts a lot for no reason at all. I call him Ants In Your Pants and often get cross with him. But when I shout at him, Mum says, "Oh Annie, don't be awkward, you know he's only little."

Huh, bet no one was ever that nice to me when I was little – I expect they told me I should be more like Posy. Just like they do now...

Chapter Two

It's just as bad at school. Everyone
thinks I'm awkward there, too.

"Why can't you be more like your
sister?" my teachers say. "She always sits
nicely and does her sums." Or, "What,
you don't know how to spell 'difficulty'
yet? Posy could do that when
she was five."

Because I'm not my sister, I want to say, but don't, because then they'll think I'm awkward too, just like my mum and dad do.

I don't think my parents mean to pick on me. And they try hard in that annoying parenty way of theirs. But really they are so dull. Mum won't even let me have my belly button pierced. How unfair is that? She says things like *Over my dead body*, and then Dad says, *Well maybe when she's eighteen*, which is another way of saying *Never*. So I say, *Can't I have my ears pierced then?* But Mum says *No you can't, young lady,* and then I say, *But everyone else has their ears pierced* (which isn't strictly true – Amy Arnold does, but then she has a mobile phone and a DVD player in her room, and I know I don't stand a hope of getting them). Dad says, *What, everyone?* and looks at me as if he is going to laugh, and then they both go, *Don't be awkward, Annie.* And that's the end of that.

Still, I suppose they aren't too bad as parents go. So long as Mum doesn't give me a kiss in the morning when she drops me at school. I've trained her well, but sometimes she forgets…

Chapter Three

I thought my family were pretty bad, and that they couldn't get any worse. But I was so wrong. Because then Great Aunt Aggie came to stay, and she is awful.

Aunt Aggie looks about a hundred. She has a wrinkly face, a pointy nose, with a wart on the end of it, and a wobbly belly. I swear she's a witch, but Posy tells me not to be so silly. She is enormously fat and plasters herself in smelly perfume that stinks of lavender. It is disgusting! And so is she. But she is Dad's auntie and Grandpa's sister so we have to be nice to her. She isn't even

that old, so Posy says. But I heard Mum say she's sixty-five, and that sounds ancient to me.

Anyway, Aunt Aggie used to live in Australia, but has come back to live in Britain for a while. And, as she has nowhere else to live, Mum and Dad said she could come and stay with us. Well, Dad said she could. Sometimes I think Mum isn't all that keen on her, because once I heard her whisper loudly to Dad when she thought we weren't listening, "She's your aunt, why don't you ask her when she's leaving?"

Another time, she told her best friend on the phone that if Aunt Aggie was still here at Christmas she was going to run away from home. But that's daft. I mean, where would Mum go if she

wasn't here? Mums don't run away from home, children do. That's the way it works in books anyway.

The thing is this though. Even though I know that Mum can't stand Aunt Aggie, and wants her to leave, if I am

the slightest bit rude to her, (like the day
I told her she shouldn't eat all the roast
potatoes as she was a big fat potato
already – which is true) I get told off.

Like I have done something wrong. One day I will be grown-up, and they will be so sorry.

Chapter Four

One day, a few weeks after Aunt Aggie arrived, she offered to take us to the park. I don't know why, because I don't think she likes children very much. Posy and I looked at each other in panic (even Posy doesn't like Aunt Aggie all that much).

"It's alright," we chorused. "We don't want to go to the park."

But Mum said yes, that would be lovely, completely ignoring our desperate pleas for mercy, as she had to do some shopping. And then Posy got out of it because her friend Creepy Clara rang up and asked if Posy wanted to come over so they could practise their times tables together.

So Aunt Aggie was left with me and my annoying little brother. I don't think Aunt Aggie is all that used to children.

So the first thing that happened is that Ants In Your Pants let go of her hand the minute we got into the park, and ran down the big hill that led to the woods. He certainly had ants in his pants that day, because he ran so fast Aunt Aggie couldn't keep up and was soon puffing crossly down the path shouting at him. In the end, she told me to go after him.

Why me? I wanted to say. *I'm just a kid. You're supposed to be looking after us.* But then she stopped by the tearoom next to the woods and blushed. At the man who was selling ice creams. I don't know why, it must be some weird grown-up thing – he was as fat and old as she was. But within seconds they were both giggling and simpering at each other,

and holding hands. It was just
DISGUSTING. They were way too old
for that kind of thing. And it looked as
though she had forgotten all about
Ant…

Chapter Five

I was feeling pretty cross as I ran down
the hill after Ant, but when I got to the
bottom he was nowhere in sight. And I
mean, nowhere. I looked up and down
the hill, but I couldn't see him
anywhere. He must have gone into the
woods. I felt a little anxious. I know he's
annoying, but he is my little brother. I
had to find him. And Aunt Aggie
wasn't going to bother. So, taking a
deep breath – this was the place that
Perfect Posy had once told me was
haunted on a rare day when she was
being mean to me – I ran into the
woods. Actually they were a little

disappointing. The woods, I mean. It was a few years since we'd been there, and I remembered them as being really dark and spooky, but there weren't even that many trees. Before I knew it, I had come out the other side, and there were lots of people wandering about. I asked everyone I saw if they had seen a little boy with fair hair running as fast as he could, and eventually someone said, "Yes, I saw him. He went down to the lake."

The lake? Didn't you stop him? I wanted to say. When we were little someone drowned in that lake. It is way deep. At least, that's what Posy always told me.

And my annoying little brother can't swim. He is only three.

I thought about running back to Aunt

Aggie, but she was probably still making sheep's eyes at the ice-cream man. She was worse than useless. Besides, I bet I can run faster than her. It was up to me.

I had to save my little brother.

So I ran and ran, as fast as I could. I ran until I felt my lungs were bursting right out of my body. And eventually I

got to the lake. I stopped and paused for breath. I couldn't see Ant anywhere. Was he already at the bottom of the lake? Maybe he had drowned already? It was my fault for not getting there fast enough.

And then I heard a faint cry, and a splash. It was my brother and he had fallen in the water.

Chapter Six

Without a second's thought – well,
maybe I did stop and think about it for a
split second, I have only just learnt how
to jump in the deep end – I ran down to
the water, put my fingers over my nose
and jumped straight in.

And landed crack on my ankles.

The lake was only about fifteen
centimetres deep around the edge, and
my brother was sitting down in the
water. He wasn't drowning, but he was
completely soaking wet.

I picked him up. I didn't care. He
hadn't drowned and that was all that
mattered. Although, of course, you only

need a few centimetres of water to drown in, so he was very lucky. If I had been a few seconds later, who knows what might have happened.

Luckily Ant thought he was having an adventure, and he didn't cry a bit when I carried him back through the woods.

I met Aunt Aggie lumbering away
from the tearoom.

"Oh, my dears, whatever happened to
you?" she said. "You won't tell your
mother, will you?"

Well, I didn't tell my mother. But plenty of other people did. It turns out there was someone from the local paper there, and he took a photo. It was in the paper and everything. You may have seen it. *Girl Saves Brother From Drowning.*

Which is pretty silly really, as Ant wasn't really in any danger. Or not much. But I suppose you never know what might have happened and it made a good story for the papers. Mum was pleased, too, because very soon after that Aunt Aggie decided to move out.

The ice-cream seller asked her to
marry him, so she was over the moon,
too. What a day that was, I can tell you.
Perfect Posy the flower girl. Annoying
Ant running around shouting like a
loony. And as for Aunt Aggie
herself, well that's a story for
another day...

And Mum and Dad kept telling me that if it wasn't for me, Ant might not be here today. Brave Bella they call me now. Which is rubbish, as I don't think he was really going to drown. But I'm not saying anything. Not one single thing. Because if I play my cards right, I might just be able to persuade them to let me have my belly button pierced before they remember that I really am Awkward Annie!

If you enjoyed this story, why not read another *Skylarks* book?

Detective Derek

by Karen Wallace and Beccy Blake

Derek was no ordinary cat. He was a cat with a difference.

If dogs could be in the police force, why not cats? So, when all the other cats were out chasing mice, Detective Derek and his partner Sergeant Norman were out on top secret police business – they were on a mission to catch the Mouse and the Boxer, the sneakiest crooks in town…

Spiggy Red

by Penny Dolan and Cinzia Battistel

Spiggy Red is sent to Planet XY73 on his first ever space mission. He must deliver a top secret casket to the famous inventor, Professor Gizmo. Spiggy sets off in his Zooper with great excitement, and everything goes well until Spiggy stops at the Lake of the Purple Pong and comes across... the Thing!

London's Burning
by Pauline Francis and
Alessandro Baldanzi

It was dark in the attic bedroom
and John really wanted a candle.
He sneaked downstairs and stole the
candle from his parents' bedroom. John
slept soundly with his candle flickering
on the windowsill beside him. But in
the morning when he woke, the air
was thick with smoke and the smell
of burning. London was on fire!
And John's candle had disappeared…

Sleeping Beauty

By Louise John and Natascia Ugliano

After a curse is placed upon her as a baby, a princess pricks her finger on a spinning wheel and falls into a deep sleep on her sixteenth birthday. The rest of the palace falls into a deep sleep with her. One hundred years later, a handsome prince rides past the forgotten palace. Will the prince be able to undo the curse and finally awaken the princess?

Skylarks titles include:

Awkward Annie
by Julia Williams and Tim Archbold
HB 9780237533847
PB 9780237534028

Sleeping Beauty
by Louise John and Natascia Ugliano
HB 9780237533861
PB 9780237534042

Detective Derek
by Karen Wallace and Beccy Blake
HB 9780237533885
PB 9780237534066

Hurricane Season
by David Orme and Doreen Lang
HB 9780237533892
PB 9780237534073

Spiggy Red
by Penny Dolan and Cinzia Battistel
HB 9780237533854
PB 9780237534035

London's Burning
by Pauline Francis and Alessandro Baldanzi
HB 9780237533878
PB 9780237534059